An account of a new poor-house, erected in the parish of Boldre, in New Forest, near Lymington, 1796.

William Gilpin

ECCO

PRINT EDITIONS

Eighteenth Century
Collections Online
Print Editions

Gale ECCO Print Editions

Relive history with *Eighteenth Century Collections Online*, now available in print for the independent historian and collector. This series includes the most significant English-language and foreign-language works printed in Great Britain during the eighteenth century, and is organized in seven different subject areas including literature and language; medicine, science, and technology; and religion and philosophy. The collection also includes thousands of important works from the Americas.

The eighteenth century has been called "The Age of Enlightenment." It was a period of rapid advance in print culture and publishing, in world exploration, and in the rapid growth of science and technology – all of which had a profound impact on the political and cultural landscape. At the end of the century the American Revolution, French Revolution and Industrial Revolution, perhaps three of the most significant events in modern history, set in motion developments that eventually dominated world political, economic, and social life.

In a groundbreaking effort, Gale initiated a revolution of its own: digitization of epic proportions to preserve these invaluable works in the largest online archive of its kind. Contributions from major world libraries constitute over 175,000 original printed works. Scanned images of the actual pages, rather than transcriptions, recreate the works *as they first appeared.*

Now for the first time, these high-quality digital scans of original works are available via print-on-demand, making them readily accessible to libraries, students, independent scholars, and readers of all ages.

For our initial release we have created seven robust collections to form one the world's most comprehensive catalogs of 18th century works.

Initial Gale ECCO Print Editions collections include:

History and Geography

Rich in titles on English life and social history, this collection spans the world as it was known to eighteenth-century historians and explorers. Titles include a wealth of travel accounts and diaries, histories of nations from throughout the world, and maps and charts of a world that was still being discovered. Students of the War of American Independence will find fascinating accounts from the British side of conflict.

Social Science

Delve into what it was like to live during the eighteenth century by reading the first-hand accounts of everyday people, including city dwellers and farmers, businessmen and bankers, artisans and merchants, artists and their patrons, politicians and their constituents. Original texts make the American, French, and Industrial revolutions vividly contemporary.

Medicine, Science and Technology

Medical theory and practice of the 1700s developed rapidly, as is evidenced by the extensive collection, which includes descriptions of diseases, their conditions, and treatments. Books on science and technology, agriculture, military technology, natural philosophy, even cookbooks, are all contained here.

Literature and Language

Western literary study flows out of eighteenth-century works by Alexander Pope, Daniel Defoe, Henry Fielding, Frances Burney, Denis Diderot, Johann Gottfried Herder, Johann Wolfgang von Goethe, and others. Experience the birth of the modern novel, or compare the development of language using dictionaries and grammar discourses.

Religion and Philosophy

The Age of Enlightenment profoundly enriched religious and philosophical understanding and continues to influence present-day thinking. Works collected here include masterpieces by David Hume, Immanuel Kant, and Jean-Jacques Rousseau, as well as religious sermons and moral debates on the issues of the day, such as the slave trade. The Age of Reason saw conflict between Protestantism and Catholicism transformed into one between faith and logic -- a debate that continues in the twenty-first century.

Law and Reference

This collection reveals the history of English common law and Empire law in a vastly changing world of British expansion. Dominating the legal field is the *Commentaries of the Law of England* by Sir William Blackstone, which first appeared in 1765. Reference works such as almanacs and catalogues continue to educate us by revealing the day-to-day workings of society.

Fine Arts

The eighteenth-century fascination with Greek and Roman antiquity followed the systematic excavation of the ruins at Pompeii and Herculaneum in southern Italy; and after 1750 a neoclassical style dominated all artistic fields. The titles here trace developments in mostly English-language works on painting, sculpture, architecture, music, theater, and other disciplines. Instructional works on musical instruments, catalogs of art objects, comic operas, and more are also included.

The BiblioLife Network

This project was made possible in part by the BiblioLife Network (BLN), a project aimed at addressing some of the huge challenges facing book preservationists around the world. The BLN includes libraries, library networks, archives, subject matter experts, online communities and library service providers. We believe every book ever published should be available as a high-quality print reproduction; printed on-demand anywhere in the world. This insures the ongoing accessibility of the content and helps generate sustainable revenue for the libraries and organizations that work to preserve these important materials.

The following book is in the "public domain" and represents an authentic reproduction of the text as printed by the original publisher. While we have attempted to accurately maintain the integrity of the original work, there are sometimes problems with the original work or the micro-film from which the books were digitized. This can result in minor errors in reproduction. Possible imperfections include missing and blurred pages, poor pictures, markings and other reproduction issues beyond our control. Because this work is culturally important, we have made it available as part of our commitment to protecting, preserving, and promoting the world's literature.

GUIDE TO FOLD-OUTS MAPS and OVERSIZED IMAGES

The book you are reading was digitized from microfilm captured over the past thirty to forty years. Years after the creation of the original microfilm, the book was converted to digital files and made available in an online database.

In an online database, page images do not need to conform to the size restrictions found in a printed book. When converting these images back into a printed bound book, the page sizes are standardized in ways that maintain the detail of the original. For large images, such as fold-out maps, the original page image is split into two or more pages

Guidelines used to determine how to split the page image follows:

• Some images are split vertically; large images require vertical and horizontal splits.
• For horizontal splits, the content is split left to right.
• For vertical splits, the content is split from top to bottom.
• For both vertical and horizontal splits, the image is processed from top left to bottom right.

AN

ACCOUNT

OF A

NEW POOR-HOUSE,

ERECTED IN THE PARISH

OF

BOLDRE,

IN

NEW FOREST,

NEAR LYMINGTON,

1796.

LONDON:

Printed at the Philanthropic Reform,
ST. GEORGE'S FIELDS.

AN

ACCOUNT, &c.

THE following account of the erection of a Poor-house, in the parish of Boldre, in New Foreſt, is intended to shew, how cheaply, and yet how comfortably, the poor of a parish may be maintained, with good management, under the present poor laws.

The old poor-house of Boldre being a wretched place, and managed without any economy, at a great expence, it was determined, at a vestry held in the year 1792, to build a new one on a better site; to put in a respectable master and mistress, and to give the overlooking of it to a monthly Committee of the gentlemen and farmers of the parish.

Accordingly they borrowed the sum of 800*l.* and bought a piece of ground, about two acres and an half, elevated, dry, and airy; here they built their house, at a little distance from the road; and yet near enough to be under the constant eye of observation. It is built substantially of brick, single, that the air may have a free passage through it, and extending about eighty-two feet in front, and twenty in breadth. These dimensions give an excellent work-room on the right, as you enter; and on the left a kitchen and back kitchen; the master's room, which is also the Committee-room, about eighteen feet by fourteen, occupies the centre, and has a window on one side, inspecting the work-room; and another on the opposite side, inspecting the kitchen; above stairs, the sleeping chambers are separated nearly as those are below; only, as there are commonly more women and children in a poor-house than men, a room at the end of the mens' apartment is taken off for a sick room, with a separate stair-case; above the chambers are excellent garrets; behind the kitchen-part of the house, are the pantries and other conveniences, among which is a store-room thirty feet long.

The ground between the house and the road, which is a falling space of about sixty yards, is divided, first into a dry convenient play-yard for the children ; and the remainder, about half an acre, running down to the road, is a garden ; the larger garden, which is about an acre, lies behind the house.

The house being thus erected, and sufficiently dry, the inhabitants of the old house, consisting of nine or ten men and women, and between twenty and thirty children, were brought into it, on the 19th of May, 1793 ; and the whole put under the care of Mr. and Mrs. Salter, whose characters will hereafter be shewn at large in the excellent management of every part of the institution.

A more disorderly set in every particular, than this family was, when Mr. Salter received it first under his care, cannot easily be conceived : when he had brought them a little into order, and shewn them it was his wish to be kind and friendly to them ; he got them, by degrees, to go on regularly in the business, and duties of the house. Both he and his wife are well acquainted with the whole business of spinning and weaving ; and having set up a couple of looms, and a number of spinning wheels, he generally presides over this part of the business himself, and Mrs. Salter over the economy and management of the house ; both departments are admirably conducted The inhabitants are all employed in that business they are most fit for : some of the old women in cooking, mending, and washing, the old men in the garden ; the children and some of the women in spinning, and weaving, children, even of four or five years of age are employed, and earn about a penny a day. In summer they come into the work-room at six ; in winter as soon as it is light ; at breakfast they have an hour's respite, and the same at dinner ; they have all tasks, which are so easy, that if they work hard, they can finish them by two in the afternoon ; but without any exertion by six.

With regard to their food; on *Sunday* they have beef, pork, or veal, as each happens to be cheapest, with plenty of vegetables, and four ounces of bread for grown persons, and three for children ; on *Monday*, they have the remains warmed with vegetables and bread ; on *Tuesday*, each grown person has a pound of pudding, and the children three quarters of a pound ; on *Wednesday*, beef, or pork, or veal, as on Sunday ; on *Thursday*, the remains as on Monday ; on *Friday*, they have generally soup made of a bullock's head, with vegetables and bread, as usual ; on *Saturday*, a clearance is made of all the remains in the house , and if they fall short, the deficiency is made up with bread and cheese ; for breakfast, beef-broth, or milk-broth is provided ; and at supper the regular meal is six ounces of bread, and an ounce of cheese for every grown person , and for children, four ounces of bread, and three quarters of an ounce of cheese ; this is some times varied with potatoes, which the children like better ; every thing is good in its kind : the children seldom eat up all they are helped to, and the remainder is fryed up again the next day among the *remains*. During the present scarcity of bread-corn, Mrs. Salter hath used a less proportion of wheat, and a larger of potatoes, particularly for supper. During the winter of the year 1795, she boiled potatoes and onions, and mixing them well together, fryed them with a little lard; the people were in general fonder of this dish than of their usual meal.

Four bushels and a half of malt are allowed each month for beer. I muft add, that the mafter and mistress generally fare as the family does, though it is not required by the Committee.

The cloathing of the poor is equally good; every one has a new suit for Sunday, generally spun and woven in the house. It is carefully hung up at night, and the old cloaths produced for the week.

Thus the poor are well lodged, well fed, and well cloathed; and yet, on deducting their earnings, at less than half the expence they cost the parish before. Their food, upon an average, is scarcely ever eftimated at so much as nine pence a head weekly; whereas in the old house, with continual complaint, the allowance was juft double;

though provisions, at that time, were much cheaper than they are now.

In the article of cloathing, much more is saved. Though the poor are now so decently clad, yet by care and management, the whole expence of the cloathing this laſt year, including shoes, amounted only to 17*l.* 6*s.* 8*d.* whereas the expence of cloathing the poor in the old house, did not amount to less, one year with another, than 70*l.* annually. In one year it reached 90*l.* And this might possibly be without any dishonesty on the part of the parish-officers, for as there was no care taken to keep the cloaths in repair, nor any distinction made between old and new, the poor were always in rags, and yet always craving for new cloaths.

Another great saving, where there is a well regulated house, is made in the article of *out-doors-poor.* There are numbers of people in every parish, who are too proud to go into a poor-house, or may perhaps be under no necessity, who are yet very ready to receive a weekly dole of a shilling, or eighteen pence a week: their plea is, if you cannot take us into a house, you must maintain us out of one. When this plea is cut off, numbers of them find the means of maintaining themselves; several indeed, under the character of *out-doors-poor*, every parish *must* maintain; but the offer of a good house draws a line between those who ought, and those who ought not to have this indulgence. In the old house the expence of the *out-doors-poor* was about 8 or 9 pounds monthly. It is at this time only 1 *l*. 12 *s*.

Another article of saving is in the health of the poor. In the other house there were often contagious fevers, and other disorders, from the closeness and nastiness of the place, and its inhabitants; and though a parish-doctor was regularly paid, yet the expence for wine and other cordials, whether necessary, or unnecessary, was often considerable, whereas the airiness and cleanliness of the present house —the good cloathing—the wholsomeness, and plenty of provisions, together with the care taken in keeping the family clean, have, under God, such an effect upon their health, that no epidemical disorder, or indeed disorder of any kind, has appeared among them. The face of the parish-doctor is hardly known.

To all these articles of saving may be added, the care and integrity of the master, and mistress. Every thing makes the best end; the very crumbs from cutting the bread for each meal are put into the milk or broth, or whatever is next prepared, and this is the more praise worthy, as neither the bread nor meat is in any shape farmed to the master; so that what he does, is done entirely from an honest principle of serving the parish. It would not indeed be difficult for him, if he were so disposed, to turn much to his own advantage; especially as he keeps the accounts of the parish, for which he is well qualified, both by his skill and his integrity.

By all these modes of care, economy, and integrity, together with the profits of the house-labour, a saving in the poor rates of the parish was made, this year, of 157 *l.* 1 *s* 6 *d.* notwithstanding the advanced price of provisions, and a variety of expences, necessary in a new establishment.

Without doors things are managed with the same care and order. Both the gardens belonging to the house are in highest degree of cultivation, and bear such quantities of potatoes, and cabbage, the chief vegetables used in the family, that the master finds he is not only sufficiently supplied, but has enough to feed his hogs, and often to give away to his poor neighbours. A theft, one night, was committed in the gardens, and at least two hundred weight of cabbages carried off. When somebody was bemoaning the loss to the master, " It was a pitiful thing, he observed, to steal from a parish work-house, but in the light of an inconvenience to him, it would have been none, if they had carried off twice as much." His ground is so well dunged, and so productive, that among a number of large cabbages, he had the curiosity to weigh one that seemed larger than the reft, and found its weight to be twenty-seven pounds, after the outside leaves had been stripped off During the scarcity of the year 1795, he was obliged indeed to purchase potatoes.

But the economy of this excellent institution is not more pleasing than the cheerful ness, and happy air, with which every thing is conducted The old women, when they behave well, have little indulgences of tea, and snuff, which they value much , the men, of tobacco , and the children's tasks are made pleasing, by giving them little gratuities out of their earnings. The master has the art of turning even their play-hours to use , and yet making them more happy, than if they were left to themselves. If he want the stones, for instance, picked out of the garden, with a small gratuity to those who pick the most, he sets such a number of little hands at work, that the business is soon accomplished , or, if he want dung brought into the garden, he yokes half a dozen of them to a wheel-barrow, and makes one of them the waggoner, with a long whip, but without the power of exercising it. This employment is very pleasing , it is good exercise, and presently dispatches the business. If the master happen to *have* no employment for them, during their play-hours, he often *makes* it. He will send, for instance, three or four of them, if the afternoon be fine, to some distant part of the parish, with a letter of no consequence, but to amuse them with a walk, and teach them to be trusty in a charge; or, in nutting-season, he will send three or four of such as he can best depend on, to gather nuts in the forest, but with condition, that whatever quantity they gather, shall be divided with those who stay at home. This year (1795) was so abundant in nuts, and such quantities were gathered, that Mrs. Salter thought it prudent to take the management of so large a store under her care, and distribute it in doles.

But none of these amusements are allowed till theirs task are performed. Sometimes in a fine morning the master signifies his intention of thus employing three or four of them: on which the wheels run with prodigious rapidity, and all business is over by two in the afternoon. He suffers them also in summer to rise very early in the morning, before the family is up, and go down quietly to their work, which they are very eager to do. Such work appears like voluntary labour. The condition on these occasions is, not to speak a word till the clock strike six, which is the appointed hour. And this condition the mas-

ter says, he believes is punctually complied
with, he often hears the whirling of the
wheels, but no other sound These little re-
straints are very useful in habituating children to order and decency.

To *exemplify* the happiness, which the in-
dividuals of this well-regulated house enjoy,
I might produce several instances, I shall
specify a few.

Two old women, reduced to the lowest degree of penury, and really starving, if their
neighbours had not assisted them, resolutely
held out, and declared that they would rather
die under a hedge, than go into the poor-
house. If such a declaration had been made
in the time of the old poor-house, they might
still have been objects of pity; but at this
time it rather cooled the charity of their
friends, who indeed thought, that maintaining them out of the house was incouraging a
discontented spirit against an institution so
well conducted, and in every light so advan-
ageous to the poor. This had it's effect;
as winter came on, and fuel grew scarce, their

pride, which had a great share in their resist-ence, gave way; and they were driven to seek the comforts of a warm kitchen fire at the house. A very short time convinced them of their folly, and they soon declared, they had never lived so comfortably before.

There was an elderly man in the parish, of the name of Brown; he had been bred a thatcher, but was able to work at any kind of labour, he was sensible, honest, and good-natured in a great degree; and being a stout, robust fel-low, he might have made a very good liveli hood; but he was so totally careless of what he earned, so thoughtless and imprudent in every respect, that he went about in rags, and never knew where to get a dinner at noon or a bed at night, indeed he had reduced him self at length to such a degree of weaknes and wretchedness, that he could hardly craw about. In this necessity, hunger at lengt drove him into the house. Here plenty o good provision soon recruited him, and he be came a useful member. To work of no kin he has objection; he digs the garden, h carries out work, he brings meat from th market, often Mr. Salter lets him out to work, on account of the parish, in thatching ricks and cottages he is particularly useful. The money he earns, he always brings honestly home; out of which he receives, for his own use, a penny in the shilling. In the mean time he is perfectly happy, he is well cloathed, well fed, and well lodged, and as to money, as he never knew the advantages of it, the want of it is no distress, the few halfpence he receives, he never keeps in his pocket longer than till he has an opportunity of distributing them among the children, and old women of the house; among whom he is so great a favourite, that the latter shew their gratitude to him by tricking him out on Sundays with all the neatness they are able. He, who used to go about the parish in rags, not worth picking off a dunghill, now goes to church in a good suit of cloaths, his breast is unbuttoned, and displays a deep ruffle hanging out, neatly plaited; his cravat is well washed; and a black ribband is tyed round his neck. His ambition and consequence were one day raised, when a stranger coming out of the church, and looking with pleasure on the orderly procession of the work-house family, pointed to Brown, and asked, If he was not the master of the house? It should be remembered however, that with all his profuseness, he was mindful, with the first money he received, to pay his debts: these amounted to four-pence, which in some pressure of his affairs he had formerly borrowed, and now remembered. This singular character, though he is so industrious, that Mr. Salter thinks he maintains at least four people by his labour, is yet so attached to the house, that nothing could prevail with him to leave it. His neighbours often tell him, what a fool he is thus to work for other people, when he might earn his own money ; but Brown is philosopher enough to know himself; and hath had sufficient experience of the extent of his own prudence, not to trust himself under its direction again, while he can live under the care of so kind a master.

But the great merit of the master and mistress of this well established house, consists in instructing the ignorant, and reforming the abandoned. Every morning, when the bell rings for breakfast, the family all assemble in the kitchen. Each knows his place, so there is no confusion, and a strict silence is injoined: soon after the master comes in, and reads, and generally explains (which he is very able to do) some easy and practical part of the New-Testament, after this they all join in prayer. On Sunday morning, and evening, these exercises are inlarged, and accompanied often with singing hymns, in which the children join. They sometimes sing hymns also at their work, when twenty or thirty spinning wheels are all going together. The master says, he would oftener introduce singing hymns at their work, but he judiciously observes, that the slowness of the measure is too apt to introduce slowness in their hands. One tune however has particular credit with him, the movements of which are well adapted to the motion of the wheel; and for that reason it goes among them by the name of the *spinning-wheel tune*; all other singing the master forbids, which appeared rather hard · his reason for it however is good, he has no objection to innocent songs, but as he found he could not draw a line between them, and such as were corrupting, he thought it necessary to forbid all together. The penalty is the forfeiture of the little earnings of the day from their labour. They regularly attend church on Sundays; and it is a pleasing sight to see so many well cloathed figures, happy faces and healthy countenances, issuing from a parish-work-house. In the afternoon, on Sunday, the children attend the school, where they are catechised with the other children of the neighbourhood the old people also attend with them.

The good order of the house is preserved rather by rewards than punishments. When this family was first received from the old house, the master had occasion for all his prudence to manage, and bring them into order. Their habits of idleness, and wickedness were so strong, and their ideas of order and discipline, so weak, that he had great difficulty in preserving the true medium between too lax, and too strict a government. If he had corrected every thing he saw amiss, he must have been continually correcting, and might have irritated, and hardened. His great art, therefore, was to find excuses for passing over many faults; and yet to make the children believe he would pass over none. When he had informed a boy, for instance, that he meant to punish him in the evening; his wife, as if ignorant of the matter, would send him to bed with the rest. In the morning he would call up the boy, and let him know, how angry he was with him, and how severely he would have punished him, if his mistress had not sent him to bed. However, as the matter was now over, he would pass it by this time. Sometimes, however, to shew he was in earnest, he would punish an extraordinary offence with severity; at the same time he endeavoured to shew that he was much readier to reward, than punish, when any thing was done which he approves. Thus by keeping a steady hand, and not hastening the work of reformation too quickly, he brought them by degrees into good order. And when he had once gotten his first set orderly, it was easy to keep up an orderly family. Such as came in afterwards, though obstinate and refractory, could not fight against so disciplined an establishment. Like headstrong bullocks yoked in an orderly team, they could not well be mischievous. As his plan is to rule rather by affection, than fear, in which he has been very successful, his punishments, when he has now brought his establisment to this orderly state, are very few, and gentle. They consist chiefly in locking up delinquents in a room by themslves, or abridging them of a meal. But these happen rarely. When he thinks himself under a necessity of punishing a boy corporally, knowing the ill-fame which masters of work-houses commonly lye under, he chooses to have some respectable person present. But he is never driven to this extremity, but in cases of theft, or other atrocious wickedness.

In this orderly house, where all bad examples are removed, and scenes only of piety, industry, and regularity are before the eye, several refractory, and some abandoned people, have been reclaimed. Among the children, it is hoped, these instructive lessons will have the best effect. But among the old people, some, who had led loose, disorderly lives, (as a forest is not the best nursery of virtue) have acknowledged themselves much happier in a state of decency, regularity, and virtue; and have accordingly changed their manners, and become orderly people; of this two, or three instances might be given.

One of the greatest instances of the happy influence of this house, in reclaiming obstinate wickedness, was shewn in a woman of the name of Young. Her father, a reprobate fellow, had been thrown into Winchester jail for deer-steeling; and as he could not pay his fine, which was thirty pounds, he was tempted to obtain his liberty, by accepting the post of county-hangman, which he held till his death. Her mother was a noisy, bawling woman, who, neglecting her family, used to beset all passengers at the bridge, and clamour loud of the hardness of the times, and the necessities of her family, two or three of whom she used generally to produce in rags, to confirm her distress. The children of such parents could hardly be supposed to turn out well. The girl, of whom we now speak, had been put to school, with a view to teach her some good, and keep her out of more harm. But it had little effect: as soon as she could use her hands dexterously, she began to pilfer, and with such ingenuity, that it is probable she had learned some lessons from her father's conversation, who had always lodgings among his old friends in the jail, during his periodical excursions to Winchester. To do him justice, however, he shewed a laudable fear, lest his daughter should come judicially under his hands; and has been known to tye her up, and correct her very severely. His severity, however, only turned her from one kind of wickedness to another. She next introduced herself to a regiment of soldiers, who were marching through the country, with whom she lived, till disease sent her back to her parish. She had now no home, her father and mother being dead. She was sent therefore to the old poor-house, which hath been described as a place not much calculated to produce reformation. When she was cured of her disorder, she went off again; leading the same profligate life she had led before, and this was repeated two or three times. In this state she was brought to the new house, which, at first was a state of uneasy confinement to her. But by degrees, the comfortable life she now led—the recollection of what she had suffered—and the scenes she had gone-through, though she was yet only a young woman, gave her mind a new turn, and she became a thorough penitent. Her credit indeed is now so great, that the master has made her one of his superintendants over the children at work.

Thus a happy, and useful society, for such it may be called, is formed out of the dregs of the parish. The old people, having all their wants well supplied, feel themselves happier than they ever did before, and are glad to render cheerfully, in return, what little services they can. And the children, bred to industry and virtue, stand a good chance of being formed, from little profligates, into useful members of society.

The parish of Boldre will long remember the humanity and integrity, the judicious management, and the religious care of the master and mistress, by whose means, chiefly, this excellent establishment has been so happily compleated.

The truth of the above particulars, is attested by the three following members of the Committee, two of whom are in his Majesty's commission of the peace for Hampshire, and the other is minister of the parish of Boldre.

JOHN WALTER.
THOMAS ROBBINS.
WILLIAM GILPIN, Vicar.

CPSIA information can be obtained at www.ICGtesting.com

231686LV00004B/39/P

9 781170 707708